Sorry for Your Troubles

Also by Pádraig Ó Tuama and published by
Canterbury Press

readings from the book of exile

Sorry for Your Troubles

Pádraig Ó Tuama

CANTERBURY
PRESS
Norwich

© Pádraig Ó Tuama 2013

First published in 2013 by the Canterbury Press Norwich
Editorial office
3rd Floor, Invicta House,
108–114 Golden Lane,
London EC1Y 0TG.

Second edition 2016

Canterbury Press is an imprint of Hymns Ancient & Modern
Ltd (a registered charity)
13A Hellesdon Park Road, Norwich,
Norfolk, NR6 5DR, UK

www.canterburypress.co.uk

British Library Cataloguing in Publication data

A catalogue record for this book is available
from the British Library

978 1 84825 462 6

Typeset by Manila Typesetting Company
Printed and bound in Great Britain by
CPI Group (UK) Ltd, Croydon

Contents

Do mo PD, le grá mór mór.

With love, respect and thanks to Susan McEwen.

A Reflection on Shaking Hands

Little did I know on the day I shook the hand of Queen Elizabeth that someone I had never met would be so inspired to pen a poem in recognition of that much publicised event. When my friend and colleague Mitchel McLaughlin drew my attention to the poem I was amazed that someone should feel so moved to compose such a wonderful poem as 'Shaking Hands'. I was intrigued – who was this person Pádraig Ó Tuama of whom I knew nothing?

Some weeks later First Minister Peter Robinson and myself were invited to speak at the Peace Centre at Corrymeela, Co. Antrim. In my speech I mentioned the poem 'Shaking Hands'. Imagine my surprise when a few minutes later I was introduced to Pádraig who, unknown to me, was among the assembled guests. I expressed my thanks and appreciation for his ability to encapsulate so effectively the symbolic significance of two people shaking hands.

I have a great admiration for poets, the works of Seamus Heaney, Patrick Kavanagh, Michael Longley and John Montague line my bookshelves. People, land, conflicts, life, love, death, hunger, reconciliation, equality, war, greed, law and loss all come under the poet's micro-scope for analysis and outcomes. Pádraig's poem 'Shaking Hands' challenges all of us on the hugely important matters of equality and leadership. Without leadership there would have been no peace process in the North of Ireland. Without equality there can be no justice anywhere.

Pádraig's latest work continues to challenge, pro-voke and advocate that a better world is not just pos-sible but essential. Honesty, empathy and compassion are the hallmarks of this work from a poet who accepts that he too has a responsibility to help make the world a fairer and better place. Maith thú a Phádraig.

Martin McGuinness
Deputy First Minister
Stormont Assembly
June 2013

Preface

Many of the poems in this book were written as responses to hearing the stories of people who lived through troubles. The poem titles have spaces between each letter as a way of indicating the importance of silence, listening, grief and the things beyond words.

Pádraig Ó Tuama

The word became stretched and crept among us

It is the tense vocation of language
to contain and constrain meaning.

Some words are better than others –
'alas' sounds nothing like keening.

Some words deepen another –
to be troubled is to be found bereaving.

It is the tense vocation of language
to contain and constrain meaning.

[t h e] n o r t h [e r n] [o f] i r e l a n d

It is both a dignity and
a difficulty
to live between these
names,

perceiving politics
in the syntax of
the state.

And at the end of the day,
the reality is
that whether we
change
or whether we stay
the same

these questions will
remain.

Who are we
to be
with one
another?

and

How are we
to be
with one
another?

and

What to do
with all those memories
of all those funerals?

and

What about those present
whose past was blasted
far beyond their
future?

I wake.
You wake.
She wakes.
He wakes.
They wake.

We Wake
and take
this troubled beauty forward.

Sorry for your Troubles

One time I sat in a comedy club in Belfast. The comedian, a gay British Asian, had the crowd in the palm of his hand. He was self-deprecating, flirtatious and hilarious. Then he said, 'What about the troubles, then? Why do you people call it that? It sounds so twee. It sounds like a spot of bother.'

Few people laughed. On the one hand, it was understandable that he would say what he said. Indeed, many peace practitioners now shy away from the word 'troubles' because of its diminutive syntactical connotations. I think that the comedian didn't know that in a room of 150 people, it is inevitable that there are people who were troubled by the troubles. Does it matter what you call something if that something is awful? The answer is yes. But the answer is also that words are never the final word.

'Don't call this war in Ireland the troubles,' a Republican man once said to me. He said, 'Some English bastard made that word up, I'm sure.' 'Do you know that for a fact?' I asked. 'No,' he said, 'but you can just tell.'

Both of these stories are stories, in some way, about English words and English-speaking people on Irish soil in Irish history. The smaller nation always lives in the shadow of the larger. The Irish word for shadow, *scáth*, is also the word for shelter. We live in the shadow and we live in the shelter of each other.

One time, I was getting a train from Dublin to Cork for a funeral. My grandfather had died as a result of an illness. I bumped into my friend Tony. 'Where are you going?' he asked. 'My granda's funeral,' I answered. 'Sorry for your troubles,' he said, and he moved on. He said it without thinking. It is what you say. In Irish, there isn't a specific word for bereavement. In English, the word 'bereave' means to deprive of, to despoil, to seize or rob. There isn't a word for this in the Irish language. Our way of saying bereavement is *trioblóid*, which, anglicised, is troubled. To be bereaved is to be troubled by grief.

We say 'I'm sorry for your troubles', or '*Is olc liom do bhris*'. We use troubles or breaking for words of bereavement. It describes the experience. We say '*comhbhrón o chroí*', meaning heart-felt-shared-sadness.

Is it Northern Ireland? Is it the north of Ireland? Tribe is demarcated and politics are discerned on simpler things than this. In the process of remembering these deaths and these bereavements we don't even have the agreed language on the name of the place where these troubled things happened. Between 1969 and 2001, 3526 people lost their lives in what has come to be known as The Troubles. This is roughly 2% of the population of [the]north[ern][of]ireland. In 2010 it was estimated that 107,000 people suffered some physical injury as a result of the conflict. The statistics people estimate that up to 500,000 people are affected by grief, ailments, or trauma following the troubles.

If we called it The Bereavements would we weigh the number more heavily?

And me? I'm just a Corkman writing poems about histories I didn't share. 'What's it like for you to live in this foreign country?' a Belfast Protestant man asked me once. That same morning a Catholic man had said to me, 'I love your city, Belfast and Cork are the two best cities, but those Dublin fellas? They're wankers.' Perhaps we are all always local and foreign to each other. Neighbour, stranger and enemy.

In the name of the neighbour
And of the stranger
And in the shadowed shelter of each other.
Amen.

One time I sat in a room with a Catholic woman whose dad had been shot dead in an ambush. She'd heard that one of the ambulance men, a Protestant, had never again been right after his shift that day.

'There's many as weren't killed that still died,' she said. And she was right.

The Facts of Life

That you were born
and you will die.

That you will sometimes love enough
and sometimes not.

That you will lie
if only to yourself.

That you will get tired.

That you will learn most from the situations
you did not choose.

That there will be some things that move you
more than you can say.

That you will live
that you must be loved.

That you will avoid questions most urgently in need of
your attention.

That you began as the fusion of a sperm and an egg
of two people who once were strangers
and may well still be.

That life isn't fair.
That life is sometimes good
and sometimes even better than good.

That life is often not so good.

That life is real
and if you can survive it, well,
survive it well
with love
and art
and meaning given
where meaning's scarce.

That you will learn to live with regret.
That you will learn to live with respect.

That the structures that constrict you
may not be permanently constricting.

That you will probably be okay.

That you must accept change
before you die
but you will die anyway.

So you might as well live
and you might as well love.
You might as well love.
You might as well love.

hunger strikers

And there was banging on the bins that night
and many frightened people woke
and noted down the hour.
The clock of hunger-strikers dead is not ignored
with ease
and 'please, God, please keep loved ones safe'
was then
repeated round and round and round
like rosaries told upon a bead,
or shoes upon the ground of orange walking.

The five demands, the five-year plan
that saw a blanket round a man,
the dirty protest, Thatcher stance,
that gave a new and startling glance
at just how deep a people's fury goes.
And God knows
each single mother's son was sick of hunger.
All those young men's faces became stripped and old,
eyes shrunk back and foreheads bold and cold,
and skin hung limp and paper thin,
barely separating blood and bone from stone.

And some did say 'enough is now enough'
and others said that 'never, never, never will a
martyr die,
he'll smile upon us long from mural's wall'.

And others said 'what nation's this?
we're abandoned on our own –
all this for clothes to warm some dying bones'
And some said 'that's a traitor's talk'
and others bowed their heads and thought that they
would hate to go that way.

Then Bobby Sands was dead
and there was banging on the bin lids on the Falls
echoed through to Shankill gospel halls.
And there was trouble on the street that night
and black flags started hanging while
people started ganging up,
black flags marking out the borders of belonging
the thin black barricade
that's been around for thirty years
and stayed a fragile point up till today and cries
of how ten mothers' sons all starved and died
when all they ate was hope and pride.

Sacramental

If there is a heaven, and I'm not sure there's not,
at its harbour will be waters that we've travelled,
sometimes seeing
mostly not.

And at its hearth will be people saying
welcome, welcome, welcome
to where you've always been a
part of.

Who knows where we started,
or how this journey ends.
All we know is that we hope in destinations
tended by the practice of these virtues –

Love, and those sacramental eyes.
Embrace with arms wise to their limitation.
Loyalty to the courage of the voice.
And wonder at these voices growing daily.

And so, we hold and bless ourselves,
in the hope of untamed harbours,
unrestrained delight
and unending love in this unfolding story.

Battlefield Bog

He paints in shapes that other people make
big rectangles, little squares
makes a canvas window
with the colours of the Irish air
earthen brown with muted green
rusty orange gleaming through the evening
hues that you could lose yourself to.

I have one time seen him singing, kneeling
in the room of his creation
watched by love and celebration
as blood rolled down his back,
surrounded by the places he has painted,
and the cracks of his acquaintance
the creative chaos that he hovers over
like a storm inside an eye
with November's greytime in the sky

Well, the moody mist was blowing over
cliffs and depths and heather, fern and clover
kissing purple back to Ulster's gentle hills
bringing us through that bad night-time
to the still of
baby-morning-eggshell-blue.

He paints in shapes with colours that are true.

Same clay

When you find the person you love, an act of ancient recognition brings you together. It is as if millions of years before the silence of nature broke, his or her clay and your clay lay side by side.
John O'Donohue[1]

We're from the same stock, you and I,
we know what it's like to mine
for our dignity in caves
we never were shown.
We remind ourselves frequently
that things as we were taught that they should be
need not necessarily be so –
like nightmares, and screaming
at careless frivolity,
grief that eats at your soul,
weddings where love was the first thing to go,
kissings and greedy eyes
drinkings and beady eyes
bastards who won't let you go.

From the same clay
the same days dawned
light on our eyes for
two decades of Erin's sweet toil.

---

1 John O'Donohue, *Anam Ċara*. London, New York: Bantam, 1997, p. 45.

We knew the green landscape
the headaches and spinnings
that gave us the legs so we ran
from the same night
the same fight
the same might not survive till our harvest is done.

We remind ourselves frequently
that life as it might just be
may not turn out to be
what we were taught from the crib –
grey days and copings with silence
and choking down years of upsurging rage.

Ah Christ, we both screamed
in our own bloody nightmares
and Christ, oh he seemed to
stay away silent,
And we both know the stilling,
the chilling, the feeling of years of
'don't talk about that till you're old'.
And we both know the crying
of tears of rejoicing at leaving
those old cares behind,
of 'tell me's' and well we
just might stay up late tonight
might finish off that wine
might toast the night while she cries.

Not yet

'You're too young
to know about The Troubles,'
the peaceman said.

And the youngman said:

fathershotdead
motherfellapart
brotherfellintohimself
otherbrothersenttolivewithothers
andmeismotheredeverything
iwasfarmedaround
andnowyearslater
wehavefoundourselvesbackbeneath
asharedandtroubledceiling.

Not yet.

No-one's too young
to know about The Troubles.

Postcards to the centre

To the centre from the edge:
This circle's marked out
by the dredges of your justice
and at these edgeplace ruts,
we eat the crusts
of hope.

Must this circle never end?
Please can we make a new shape
shaped a bit like you and shaped like me
shaped like how we think that things might be
if things were not the way they've been.
And yes, I know, that's a dreamer's dream
but sometimes dreams, like nightmares,
can be real.

To the centre from the edge:
We're still here.
If you drown out all our voices.
you will not drown out your fear.
We're still here.

To the centre from the edge:
We will live with you
if you will live with us.
You go first
and then we'll follow.

You start off today,
and we'll catch up
tomorrow.

To the centre from the edge:
Can we lay down arms
refuse to fire them?
Even though we've sold our rightarms
to acquire them?
If we stop
before we're finished
will we emerge unfinished
or defeated?
Can we carve out some radius of peace
and will we need to fight to keep it?

To the centre from the edge:
We describe the centre
by our edgeplace
habitation.
We inscribe the middle
with invisible
lamentation.

Now we're issuing an invitation:
Drink our tears
and we'll drink yours.
Show your fears
and we'll show ours.

g o t o h e l l

he is called to hell, this man
he is called to glory.
he knows well those twisted ways
and those who've lost their story.

he is called to clay, this man
he is called to yearning.
he has heard of hidden streams
that heal those tired of burning.

he's searching out those raised in hell.
he wants to know the things they know.
he believes in dreamland.
where the raggéd people go.

he is called to quiet now.
he is called to silence.
squat down on the breaking ground
with those who've swallowed violence.

he is called to anguished thoughts.
he is called to flowers
to find in hell's own lonely fury
that which no flame devours.

i saw him on the midway path
i saw he carried two things only.
on his trip to hell, this man,
he is called to story.

Babel

And then our towering pyre
burned like the fire of babel.
The little gods we'd tried to be
had been vying with each other,
had been smothering our breathing
with their seething rage.
We'd even made the places of our praying
fall prey to smoke and ashes.
And so we watch as our altar crashes
toward the ground.

So now we're found on earth
surrounded by our neighbours
and the trees
and on the tree is crucified a child
and on that child is the rot of all our
fear
and inside our fears are buried
years
and years
and years.
And so we stand.

We are woman
we are man
we are just one human
we know life and death

and life-in-death is barely worth the living.
So we stand holding hands with hope
seeking wisdom and seeking meaning,
exposing what we're feeling,
and what we're feeling
is the anchoring of argument
in the shared ground of
our hope.

We can find our sanity at
the table of our talking.
We can shape our future
if we keep on with our walking.
We can walk forever if we listen to our stories.
We can tell our stories
if our stories find a home.

Welcome to Belfast

In my first week living in Belfast I looked out my back window and saw a small boy, wrapped in an Irish flag, standing on my back wall. He was singing a song.

My back wall looked over a peacewall, a 20-foot barbed wire covered construction that keeps neighbourhoods from neighbourhoods. His flag was green, it was white and it was orange. Green for Catholics, Orange for Protestants and the White in between, perhaps, for absence.

On the other side of the wall, were houses homing Protestant people. But in the inbetween space between my backwall and the peacewall, there was a stretch of land that used to be a school field. The school was empty and the pitch was overgrown. The words of his song moved across the weeds and the sportsground. They echoed through the empty rooms of a school. His words were the breath covering the land that was unused. His words bounced against the peacewall. They echoed back. I wonder if any spilled over.

His song said 'Burn, burn, burn ye bastards.' He repeated its alliterative assault, his little fist pumping and his sharp voice carrying across an empty field. There are houses there now.

What made him sing his song? Nobody seemed to be watching him. Who did he think he was singing to? Who did he think he was singing for?

There is no action without an equal but opposite reaction. I learnt that in my physics class when I was a teenager. It was early morning on an August Sunday in 2003 and there were bonfires being built to commemorate the republican men who were interned in the 1970s. Internment-remembering bonfires burn the Union Flag in an equal but opposite reaction to the Boyne-remembering bonfires burning the Irish Tricolour. It felt as predictable as the seasons and as dependable. The only motion is on an axis of its own.

A few days later, when the fires were high and as yet unlit, with Union Flags waiting to be burnt, some brave Protestant boys snuck into the field and stole that flag. I don't know how they scaled the peacewall with its sharp cutters. They climbed in, and while beer was being drunk in by the fire-lighters, these Protestant boys stole their flag back. It was a game of capture the flag. It was a game of loyalty and loyalism. It was a game of pluck and danger. It wasn't a game at all. I watched them from my back window. Thank God they weren't caught. Later that night, the fires were reflagged and they burnt in that tired old schoolfield.

The fire cracked my window.

The Opposite of Fear

There is a small boy standing singing
on a wall, and his song says:
Burn, burn, burn ye bastards,
Burn, burn, burn ye bastards,
Burn, burn, burn ye bastaaaaaards,
Ear-lye in the morning.

When I was a small boy, I wondered what to do
with all those Drunken Sailors.
There were so many of them.
And when I found that Long-boats don't make
sober sailors,
I searched out new tactics to silence them –
Cowering,
Singing Other Songs,
Long Walks.
I even put myself in a Long-boat and
sailed to the Pacific . . .
But they know how to follow.

Who has taught us to fear, my little man?

You, in your four-foot-frame, carry lusty barricades
against those on the other side of our
barbed-wire Peaceline,

– those who you do not want to love you,
– those you do not dare to care for,
for, oh what songs would you be left with then?

And me . . . I thought I'd perfected all my sailings
and my singings,
but the distance is getting shorter now.
I am a Protestant on the Falls
and a Catholic on the Shankill
of my own fearings,

and may we learn to love.

The Pedagogy of Conflict

I
When I was a child,
I learnt to lie.

When I was a child
my parents said that sometimes,
lives are protected
by an undetected
light lie of
deception.

When I was a child,
I learnt to lie.

Now, I am more than twenty five
and I'm alive
because I've lied
and I am lying still.

Sometimes
it's the only way of living.

II

When I was a child
I learnt that I could stay alive
by obeying certain
rules:

let your anger cool before you
blossom bruises on your brother's shoulder;

always show your manners at the table;

always keep the rules and never question;

never mention certain things to certain people;

never doubt the reasons behind
legitimate aggression;

if you compromise or humanise
you must still even out the score;

and never open up the door.
Never open up the door.
Never, never, never open up the blasted door.

When I was a child,
I learnt that I could stay alive
by obeying certain rules.
Never open up the door.

III
When I was a child,
I learnt to count to five
one, two, three, four, five.
But these days, I've been counting lives, so I count

one life
one life
one life
one life
one life

because each time
is the first time
that that life
has been taken.

Legitimate Target
has sixteen letters
and one
long
abominable
space
between
two
dehumanising
words.

Childsplay

Doctors and Nurses
Mummies and Daddies
Teachers and Pupils
of fear.

A game that was played
on the carpets of home
a game that they grew up
believing

leaving no place for grieving
or crying or shame,
a game that was centred
on the pure skill of blame.

They played Doctors and Nurses
that were midwifing fear,
they played Mummies and Daddies
with their hands on their ears,
they played Teachers and Pupils
with the rod in the hand,
and if they hear the wrong answer
they'll stand and demand a
rich ransom.

These games that were learned
at the high kitchen table

you knew who you hated
before you were able to ask what it meant –

childsplay forgotten,
innocence rotten and made disappear,
there are places for childhood,
but those places aren't here.

Telling Secrets

I've been told a secret
and I'm told I cannot break it
or I will make it worse

and God only
knows
what happens then.

It'll be my fault
and I'll be to blame
I will be the origin of this family's shame.

I've been taught a language,
I've been taught the things to say
and the things that make a bomb diffuse
these complex rules of conflict:

You step over here and don't mention death,
step under there, and take a left at
the place called truth and feeling.

And I've been needing
safety
but I fear it's far away.

There are hidden secrets hanging from the ceiling,
and the scene is closed and curtained up,
the scene is not for speaking or for grieving.

But I've been breaking secrets
I've been telling tales
I shouldn't tell.

I've been staring hell straight in the face.
and I've been making noises in a place
that's meant for silence.

I've been shouting peace in a place of quiet conflict.
Because I was bearing weights
far too heavy for my shoulders.

And I was young, I was not very old.
So I've been telling secrets
that I shouldn't have been told.

Firewhiskey

Walking through the last part of the night,
still humming with sleep
and unwoken dreams,
I wear a heavy coat and have not yet spoken.
Others journey too – I do not know them, but
see them often – silent in these early hours,
and I give a nod,
a recognition of some common kind of hunger
that brings us
here.

Sometimes unwashed,
smelling of last night's sweat
and late endings,
we, the scarf-bundled, stand in our anoraks and pray.
We make signs of old habit,
and start the day again,
with bread,
and blood, like firewhiskey, burning down our throats,
the early softsharp intake of alcohol and hope all
mingled.

And when we leave,
with hands and head and gut and chest and breast
still wet with second-hand water,
dabbed, still dripping,
for peace and protection,

we salute the crone.
She is a living sign of giving
here among the meaning-seeking.

Outside, the night has not yet ended
and the dawn has just begun,
we are wrapped in humdrum,
wrapped in the halfdank halflight
from this other side of twilight.

Bury the Hatchet

I heard of a woman who was shunned out of her community in Belfast. She had an hour to pack a life and leave. She had two children. She didn't know where to go and a white van turned up from Corrymeela. The driver said, 'I'll take you somewhere safe.' And having no other option, she piled her bags, her children, what of her life she could take and her very own self into the van.

Not knowing who or what Corrymeela was, she also took a hatchet.

Corrymeela began as a place of peace in a place of deepening division. Ray Davey, its founder, had been an army chaplain during the second world war and was captured and held in Dresden where he witnessed the Allied Forces' bombing of that very same city. He could no longer think of sides. When he returned to Belfast he began the dream-making behind the Corrymeela Community, an open village, a place of safety where people of diverse identities, politics, religions and viewpoints could gather for learning, community and faith. There were some nights in the 1970s when they slept scores of people whose own homes had been made unsafe.

What happened to the hatchet? I'm sure she kept it. I met a man who said that when there was trouble on his street, he slept on the upstairs landing, in front of his children's bedroom doors. He slept with a hatchet. He slept, armed, for their safety.

The folks of Corrymeela have long believed that human encounter between people who believe and think different things can have a transformative effect. Transformative because it is more courageous to have an argument with a person in a room than never entering that room in the first place. Transformative because when you can be in a place of beauty it might be that your mind can be open to new and creative possibilities, and because to lighten the shadow of our land, we must all speak of our own shadows. Transformative because when you have an ethic that challenges scapegoating, you may be able to open up a way of reflecting on your own shortcomings. Transformative because they believe in the power of the shared table and the poured cup of tea. Morning meetings start late in Corrymeela, because they know that there are some conversations that can be only take place in the dark, by firelight.

Many of the poems in this book were written following participation in encounter groups where adults met and spoke with each other, run by Corrymeela, or East Belfast Mission. One woman got up once, and left the room because a question had been too difficult. When she came back, another woman said, 'I cry in the bathroom too.' It was an acknowledgement, a solidarity, a sharing of the ground. It was also a containing kind of kindness. It helped her hold herself together. People spoke of enjoying being chased by police in the riots, a blind woman spoke of walking up roads with permanent potholes, an art teacher spoke of the prisoner who used to paint the flowers from the still life class every day until they died, women spoke of being divided by a large green gate, and finding new stories when they practised the language of fruitful disagreement.

People come from other places too, many from places of conflict. One time, a roomful of people were asked when they first became aware of conflict in their society. They told stories of five-year-old wisdom, six-year-old horror, seven-year-old lessons. They told stories of learning to lie so that your daddy's police job wouldn't be known. They told stories of parents lying in order to keep a semblance of order. They told stories about guns under beds, about knowing why you don't go out at night, and stories about playing doctors and nurses for bomb victims. We had artists and poets there, responding to the stories. The art does not stop the story, or even heal the story, but it can create a marking, bear some witness, honour the truth-time of the story told.

The Corrymeela Community believes that the quality of the telling of a story will be related to the quality of the listening of the people. There is no shortcut to human encounter. Susan McEwen told me this. So, she makes sandwiches and space and tea and provides tissues for the talking spaces that she holds, and she holds them well. She curates encounters with a careful tone. She's the one who invited poets and artists to listen. And she tells us that we must listen well. Etymology hints at some words in the hidden fabric of the word 'story'. We hear echoes of words that have been used to speak of the wise people and echoes of words that mean seeing. To tell a story means to see wisely. It is wise to speak of grief. It is wise to not rush hope. It is wise to not end a story before it is ended. It is wise to listen. It is wise to see. A blind woman took part in a long-term story project once and she told us of how she saw The Troubles. She used the word 'saw' and she laughed at us. She had had a landlady who used to follow and watch for her safety when she, independent and confident, walked down roads that were known for hostility. She walked bravely and she heard and saw what was really going on.

Once, in a room, a person spoke about having taken a life. These words were carefully chosen. Another spoke about a war. Another spoke about legitimate targets. Others said that some things are regrettable but that the story was bigger than blame. Others said that they live every day with the truth of their doing. Language is so loaded and in the middle of it all, one man used his words to name the names of people he'd bereaved. Parent. Sister. Friend. Partner. Children.

Another time when I was travelling, I met Ali Abu Awaad from the Parents' Circle, a forum for bereaved Israeli and Palestinian family members. It was Good Friday and I had hoped to pray but couldn't find the concentration. Ali, chain smoking, spoke in his third language with dignity. He told stories of humanity and generosity. He told a story of his dead brother and a story about finding friends in unexpected places. After that, I didn't feel the need to pray, as Ali had done it for me. I felt the need to tell him this, to tell him that his telling had sacramentalised this holy hallowed hollow day. But when I tried to tell him this, looking out over the hills of Beit Sahour, I just cried and couldn't stop. He put his hand on my shoulder and whispered, 'I'm not a very good Muslim,' and I laughed and said, 'I'm not a very good Catholic.' We stood and looked over the beloved hills.

One woman said that she wasn't sure if meeting people from the other side was going to be kind. She'd lost three members of her family, she said, and she wondered if the folks she'd be meeting would be embarrassed to meet someone like her, the pitiable victim of a national cause. Another man said that when he was sentenced to inhuman jail time, he wondered what had happened to the humanity of the judge.

The Irish word for forgiveness is *maithiúnas*. It comes from the word *maith*, meaning good. The word is the same, or similar, in Cymraeg, Gaelg and Gàidhlig – other languages spoken across the islands of Britain and Ireland. To forgive someone is 'to good' them. To forgive someone is to treat them with the goodness with which they did not treat you. Curiously, this syntax arranges power as the possession of the troubled one. It is they who can good, and if the one whose hands caused the trouble asks for forgiveness, they say '*maith dom*', 'good me'. Forgiveness is not a person, place or thing. Forgiveness, like priesthood, if it is to be anything, must be a verb.

Mind you, it isn't the only way to pack up your troubles. Forgiveness can be a burdening thing too and there are many good ways to honour bereavement. For some, forgiving is too much like forgetting, no matter what we say. I wouldn't argue with them. So they pour pure energy into justice, story finding, body finding and survival. Maybe that hatchet doesn't need to be buried. Maybe it can be used – to fell a tree, to clear a path, to build a house, to shine, to be proud of.

In the beginning

The people lived in darkness
and the darkness overcame them.

And isn't it true for all of us

and isn't it true for all of us
that we need someone
to watch us when we leave
and when we need
to make our own
way home,
and
when we're making something we can't see,
or when we're shaping up to be
a person that can feel
a hundred sorrows and still
get through the day
who could dream a hundred horrors
and make it anyway,

isn't it true for all of us
that we need a guiding
other,
maybe mother, maybe lover,
maybe nothing other than a stranger,
who could see our fear,
and with kindness then, unfold a welcome,

isn't it true for all of us
that we need our secrets told
and that without another
to bear witness to the children
that were never born,
and would never be a grown-up
we would be alone and lost and cold,
there would be childish hungers left
inside of us,
needing to grow old.

The Sash

Up close, it smelt familiar
and the scent of warm, worn leather
brings to mind the tent, the field, the drive, the men,
the weather always sunny in July.

The feel was festive,
fringed with old traditions kept alive
tattered endings, like curtains in a window
through a wall.

The sash picked up the smell of sweat and marching
as a man walked on his way,
purple badged and marking stages of
his faith and pride and history.

A playing band was hired
to lead him on his summer day
through Springfield ways and Barricades.
There were men brought in to play
or stage a demonstration
marching music marking
out the smells of segregation.

Up close, we smell familiar
skin and warmth and bed and clothes and home
all bring to mind
a body's hopes
and fearings for her home.

Men in a war

Men in a war
prefer the talk of
politics
than of
pain.

Girl in a blitz

Born indoors
in nineteen twenty nine
from the time that I was five

I was proudly knocking doors
to see a baby born alive,
or a body laid out on the freshly laundered sheets

arm in arm with my wee chum
poking people lying for their wake
and babies waking crying for their mum.

And that was us,
oh, we were brave and young,
appropriately unstung by death.

'Sorry for your Troubles'
we'd learnt to say
like all those local ladies.

Me and her, knees kept warm
by long brown socks,
rock solidly protected from war's cold knocks.

My mother took me by the hand
and walked me down
to the short strand.

Tully McGee is dead, they said
wrapped in a brown shroud
laid out on his own bed.

No empty hands arriving
at a house of grief
always one arm longer than the other.

My mother took along her cake
and jammy sandwiches, and me
a girl before a war.

Then the sirens broke into our night
and bundled me, my nightie, frightened
with my teddy and all my family

into a shelter stark and cold.
Belfast's Prods and Taigs and me
with my legs shaking

making games up in my mind
trying, trying, trying to find
games that are suited for the dark.

Mother praying while the blitz rained down

While the rosary was clicking
I noticed my mum's
slip
was sticking
out.

She was
such a private woman;
wouldn't countenance
going out
without
a hat and shawl on.

I remember
in the shelter
she was on
her knees.
And while the bombs
rained freely
down,
she was
salve-regina-ing
for the
pieces of her
prudence.

This is the word of the Lord

Some learnt the bible-books
like they were 'a, b, c'
while some learnt communion prayers
like they were 'do-re-mi'.

Some learnt with fuzzy-felt
old and two-dimensional
others learnt by living lives
bold and unconventional.

Some learnt by negligence
and falling on their knees
and scraping skin and feeling guilt
and going where they pleased.

Some learnt by ignorance
some learnt by prayer
many learnt by surviving hate
under priestly stares.

Some have heard of difference
and Judas Maccabees.
Others heard that Mary was
differently conceived.

Some caressed those skin-thin pages
early every morning.
Others learnt of sin and death
and hell and early warnings.

Some learnt Corinthians
others made confession.
Both crossed the green peacegate
seeking out new lessons.

Troubles in the concrete and field

Walking blind from the roundabout
up the Grosvenor,
there are no footpaths,
no road-markings
no signs to guide safe crossing,
here where colleagues go silent
when the talk turns to funerals,
unless they're crying
for their shot-face Juliet
dead in the hand of her lover,
hand still warm where he held onto her.
Children taught to make guns
out of crutches
while men,
wiser and more beaten than they know,
make crutches from those guns
trying to learn to walk again,
but always ready to defend.

And these are not just city troubles
they belonged to country air
just as much as Belfast clay.
Their smell reached rural noses too,
like burning that farmer's hay
on that day of his brave gesture.
The death of the fodder of his land.

That poor man's family had to
watch him while his face went grey.
And when tribal tags were washed
from a farmland wallway,
codes were called,
and gunmen watched from branches,
up those trees we've grown accustomed to
the trees that grew and grew and grew
till we couldn't see beyond them.

How did we allow this to happen?
The watching and the fearing?
Painting a dying flower
not rearing it in life?

Clan

We are not children any longer
yet the feelings seem stronger now
than they did then.

We were adults making choices
we didn't want to make.
Unexpected deaths brought
responsibilities in their wakes.

A war was an event we
survived with surprising wonder
We sang and cried through all these things
with words we learnt when we were younger.

The family's home, the family's land.
The family's name and place.
The family's grief, the family's need.
Their cruelty and hunger.

We carry these, through all our years
We've decided what we'll become.
Carrying people, Needing people,
People becoming one.

Once upon a timebomb

The stories we've told
were carefully moulded
with not-so-lightly chosen
terminology.

Words avoided
and what was told aloud
was certainly not as loud
as what was shrouded
by our mutually unagreed silence

because violence,
while it is deep in us,
is not what sleeps deepest in us.

And the question is
can I see my face
when I face my own history
from where you've faced it?

And the question is
can we create the space that holds us
and moulds us in our bodies
so that we embody
who and what
we can be
with one other?

Mixed marriage

There's no place like home
but home's not where I am
home is where I'm safe and sound
home is where my family's grand.

There's no place like home
and I've lived in a house.
I got married across the fence
and I've been called a tout.

And my Protestant friend beside me
saved me from a petrol bomb
me with a wee one, six weeks old
my neighbour's love kept me from harm.

There's no place like love
and my love's mixed and matched.
Him from a Protestant and British stock
and me from the Irish and Catholic stash.

Conversation starters

Do you remember when you could read the troubles
by the nearness of the choppers?
And if the coppers looked aggressive or looked calm.

One time, long ago, I thought I loved
a man whose hands were big and meaty
later on, I found out that he had
eaten with the other side once a week or more.

I remember crying while I was lying on the floor.
I remember thinking
'I just don't know if I can cope with any more of this.'

Half a lifetime later,
there were men both grown and young
gunned
on a Wednesday at the bookies.
Five men died and another dozen hearts were
frozen.
They lived cold and lonely lives from then
and when I'd see them,
Jesus, I would wish that I could see them warmer.
Three dead from the drink
and another one's a former user,
keeping on the wagon now, thank God.

And we loved a game of chasies from the peelers in
the riots
We loved to hear the peace and quiet broken
with a bottle burning smallfire,
Small Seanie was a flyer,
you couldn't catch him if you tried,
He's grown man now,
he lost his son and he watched his wife decide to die,
slowly,
like all the other unrecorded murders in the dark.

And bloody hell, this life's been stark,
but I'm alive,
and I have started telling out my story,
and I'm not the only one who's suffered,
and I'm not the only one
who's found a way of living kindly.
Conversation has been finding me finding that
tea and grief share well around a table.
Even all those yawning years of sadness
can't stop the powerful feeling that I'm glad
this talking has begun.

In the beginning, part II

The people lived in darkness
and the darkness overcame them
for a while.

The people learned to cope
so they spoke little of the things that
they had hoped for.

They learned to escape
so they took breathing breaks
in the bathroom.

The people lived in the here-and-now
they stayed here-and-now in corners
previously unfound in two-up-two-down houses.

The people learned to walk.
The people stood and they survived.
The people learned to live without

the lives that had been taken.
Their only choice was that they stand
so therefore they stood shaken.

The people chose their crutches
carefully carved and chosen:
a bit of drink,

a bit of soap TV,
a weekly visit to a friend's house
for cups of tea and paracetamol.

The people's throats are choked with
lives that are not living
and the thing about it is

that they have coped
with things that
they should not be roped with.

The people are victorious,
they can look you in the eye
and size you up.

Their hold on life is
loose
and their embrace is tight.

The people stood in darkness
and in it
they've become their light.

The Queen's Irish

Gráinne Ní Mhaille was the chieftain of the Ó Maille clan in the sixteenth century. She was a pirate and known as the Sea Queen of Connaught. The anglicised version of her name, Granuaile, can be translated as 'Bald Gráinne'. When she was a child she wished to sail with her father and he said she couldn't as her hair would get caught in the ropes of the ship.

So she cut her hair off.

When her sons were captured by the English governor of Connaught she sailed to England to meet Elizabeth I. It is said that she concealed a dagger in her gown. It is said that she blew her nose on the handkerchief of a lady and then threw that lace-edged handkerchief into the fire. Neither Gráinne Ní Mhaille nor Elizabeth I were mild. It is said that between them there was a powerful kinship, or, perhaps, a kinship of power. Neither bowed to the other. Neither spoke the first language of the other. They spoke in Latin. They made demands that were agreed upon but never met.

In 2011, Mary McAleese, the President of Ireland, welcomed Elizabeth II to the Republic of Ireland. It was the first visit of a British Monarch since Elizabeth II's grandfather, 100 years before, when Ireland was considered to be British Sovereign Territory. Here, too, were two powerful women. And they spoke in the language of gesture. Upon greeting each other, they went to stand at the Garden of Remembrance in Dublin, laid a wreath and bowed while a poem was read remembering those Irish people who had died in the fight for survival and independence.[2]

> *I ngeimhreadh na daoirse rinneadh aisling dúinn.*
> *Mheileamar sneachta táimhe.*
> *Agus rith abhainn na hathbheochana as.*
> *Chuireamar ár n-aisling ag snámh mar eala ar an*
> *abhainn.*
> *Rinneadh fírinne den aisling.*
> *Rinneadh samhradh den gheimhreadh.*
> *Rinneadh saoirse den daoirse.*
> *Agus d'fhágamar agaibhse mar oidhreacht í.*

In the winter of bondage we saw a vision,
We melted the snow of lethargy,
And the river of resurrection flowed from it.
We sent our vision aswim like a swan on the
river,
The vision became a reality,
Winter became summer,
Bondage became freedom,
And this we left to you as your inheritance.

---

2 Liam Mac Uistin, 'We Saw a Vision'. This poem is inscribed in the stone wall of the monument in Dublin's Garden of Remembrance in Irish, English and French. Written in *aisling* style, an ancient form of Irish poetry, it was the winning entry in a competition in 1976 for a suitable poem for the venue. The quoted lines are only the final section of the poem.

There are many things that have been said about whether gestures between the privileged are worthwhile or worthless. Perhaps the extremities of these categories are themselves unhelpful. Both leaders are representatives of powers that some take pride in and others lament. They represent two stories in the aim to have nonpartisan heads of state in a democratic system. Neither story is perfect; some love and some hate them.

I was unprepared for emotion. I was curious. I was astonished at seeing a British Queen's head bowed in a place that remembered Irish freedom. When she stood up at the formal dinner in Dublin Castle, I wondered which language she would address the gathered in.

English or Irish?

Or Latin?

Isn't Irish just English spoken with a funny accent? We have all heard so often. There is no word for 'no' in Irish. So we say *ní hea* – it is not.

'*A Úachtaráin agus a cháirde*,' she began, using the formal code of address that has informality at its heart. 'President and friends'.

Never has a greeting been so meaningful. They clapped in their seats in Dublin Castle. You can hear the *Úachtaráin* say wow, a word beautifully appropriate in its literal political incorrectness.[3] I cried in my armchair in Belfast

---

3 http://cdn.thejournal.ie/media/2011/05/20110518queen.mp3

watching the coverage on the television. While gesture is not the final word, it is a fine first word.

The next year, Elizabeth II came to Belfast towards the end of the celebrations of her Jubilee year. Sinn Fein had indicated that Martin McGuinness, the Deputy First Minister in the Northern Ireland Assembly, was open to meeting her. Depending on your viewpoint, the question as to who was doing the more generous task was weighted. Each is called leader by many. Each may see the other as a face of opposition, oppression even. Each has been bereaved, troubled by grief. One may be called a freedom fighter, or a terrorist-turned-politician. One may be called a beloved Monarch, or the representative of 700 years of English involvement in Ireland.

They did not meet at a Jubilee event, instead they met at an arts event run by Co-operation Ireland, a charity I had worked for. I was asked along, asked to dress well, asked to content myself with drinking coffee and eating croissants while historic handshaking occurred on the periphery of the gathering. I was happy to be there. My curiosity had deepened. I dressed well, an unusual occurrence. I made sure to button more buttons on my shirt than I normally do, and I wondered, 'What does a handshake mean? Who will love what they are doing? Who will hate it? What do I think of participating in an event like this when I neither love nor hate either? How will I address them? In what language?'

They shook hands. She in a gloved hand, with him in an ungloved one. They met with the gathered artists. I greeted each – the Deputy First Minister, the

Queen and Michael D. Higgins, the newly elected Irish President – in their own language. I had been taught well that language contains a power.

Robert Frost stated that in order to be universal, poetry must be parochial. The word 'parish' can trace its etymology to the Greek word *parousia*, which can mean exile. Who is most in exile in the northern corner of Ireland? I think of people I have met, people for whom neither hands nor lives stop shaking. I think of people disenfranchised by a binary system that amputates. I think of stories silenced, and ambiguities deliberately ignored. So, I wrote a poem about shaking and hands. Martin liked it, and I found him as likeable. I had always liked Michael D. And I pay a linguistic debt of tears, honour and thanks to the Queen and her Irish. I deepened my critical and complicated admiration for those whom we call our leaders.

Troibloidí na Sasanach[4]

'Are you from Northern Ireland?' the English woman said to the Belfast Protestant woman. 'I am,' she said. 'My son was killed a few years ago,' the English woman said. 'I just wanted to tell you that. I just needed to tell you that. I miss him. He was so young. We miss him. We miss him.'

---

4 The bereavements of the English.

After the war

After the war
there was
silence
and we heard
things our
violence could
not end.

The quiet wind
the lapping
water.

After the war
we cried, then,
most sadly.
Oh me, oh my.
We have lost
what we thought we
so badly needed,
all that we fought for
and now are left
aware and
bare, and
shameful.

After the war
there was then

no more
of us, of me
left for fighting
as we lay
sadly down
and looked.

After the war
we sang badly,
with broken hands
upon our
breasts.
Oh Lord
Oh Lord
may we not
forget.

Flags

to flutter, to grow weary, to mark a place with stone
to flutter, to grow weary, to mark a place with stone
to flutter, to grow weary, to mark a place with stone

in war, and death, in hope and in memory
in war, and death, in hope and in memory
in war, and death, in hope and in memory

our land, our street, our neighbourhood, our territory
our land, our street, our neighbourhood, our territory
our land, our street, our neighbourhood, our territory

1916, 69, 98 and today
1916, 69, 98 and today
1916, 69, 98 and today

it's only colours, coloured fabric, a construction, not an end
it's only colours, coloured fabric, a construction, not an end
it's only colours, coloured fabric, a construction, not an end

but it's beautiful and it's broad and it's our blood and it's our home
but it's beautiful and it's broad and it's our blood and it's our home
but it's beautiful and it's broad and it's our blood and it's our home

and they're our colours, our histories, our boys who'll not return
and they're our colours, our histories, our boys who'll not return
and they're our colours, our histories, our boys who'll not return

to flutter, to grow weary, to mark a place with stone
to flutter, to grow weary, to mark a place with stone
to flutter, to grow weary, to mark a place with stone

oh beckon us beyond these borders of our belonging
oh beckon us beyond these borders of our belonging
oh beckon us beyond these borders of our belonging

Left, left, left right left
Left, left, left right left
Left, left, left right left

Ikon

i
every word becomes
meaningless when over
explained, the
real meaning fades
grows dim
illuminating darkness in the
nook of disappointment. oh god, we are
groaning for release.

ii
if I demand your hand, and if I
command a feeling, I have
ordered love to fake some meaning. these days, I am
needing something different, an invitation, because
imitation leaves me dry and thirsty, I am coming close
to bursting, I am
coming close to worshipping my ragged self.

iii
a priest
prepares his preaching,
opens up his teaching books and
casts his looks toward heaven.
all the while, apocalypse is
looming, like vessels booming underneath his skin.
yearning for some inkblood on some paper.

preach it with precision pater!
take us from this unknown home
invite the only selves that we can be
change us in this empty place of feeding.

iv
here are my two hands,
empty, but for strands of hope
remaining from the days when I
easily imagined I could hold the
truth. a breeze of harsh reality
is the thing that blew and
changed my tune,
and I present you now with failing
love amidst the ruin of my truthing.

v
fucked it up again
and there are two things that
I need, and three things that I'm
longing for, not much. a little
intimate encounter with another
needing shelter in this harvest of our
greed. oh god, I need belonging.

In the image of god

In the image of god
the text tells a god
and god tells god
telling god telling god.

And with each telling
the image comes closer
and rhymes a little more
with the sounds from the mouths
of our own hungry bodies.

And god wrote god
writing god writing
god.

So we say no
because we know
that someone
somewhere
said no too.

In the echo of a man
the text tells a voice
and the voice tells a story
so the story sounds like god.

We are not the same

We are not the same.
If we think we are
we end up playing games
where dignity's dependent
on some flimsy proof.

We must know this truth:
dignity's not a game
that can be won or lost
because winners always define glory
and losers always suffer loss.

Rather, we are us.
Not because of anything
just because, just because
just because everything
less than this
demeans us.
Anything less than this
depletes us.

And in this space of sharing
there are various
types of people
loving people
loving people.

And while we're not the same
our intrinsic worth is equal.
We are less
if we accept
anything less than equal.

Shaking Hands

27ú lá Meitheamh, 2012

Because what's the alternative?
Because of courage.
Because of loved ones lost.
Because no more.
Because it's a small thing; shaking hands; it happens every day.
Because I heard of one man whose hands haven't stopped shaking since a market day in Omagh.
Because it takes a second to say hate, but it takes longer, much longer, to be a great leader.
Much, much longer.

Because shared space without human touching doesn't amount to much.
Because it's easier to speak to your own than to hold the hand of someone whose side has been previously described, proscribed, denied.
Because it is tough.
Because it is tough.
Because it is meant to be tough, and this is the stuff of memory, the stuff of hope, the stuff of gesture, and meaning and leading.
Because it has taken so, so long.
Because it has taken land and money and languages and barrels and barrels of blood and grieving.

Because lives have been lost.
Because lives have been taken.

Because to be bereaved is to be troubled by grief.
Because more than two troubled peoples live here.
Because I know a woman whose hand hasn't been shaken since she was a man.
Because shaking a hand is only a part of the start.
Because I know a woman whose touch calmed a man whose heart was breaking.
Because privilege is not to be taken lightly.

Because this just might be good.
Because who said that this would be easy?
Because some people love what you stand for, and for some, if *you* can, *they* can.
Because solidarity means a common hand.
Because a hand is only a hand; so hang onto it.

So join your much discussed hands.
We need this; for one small second.
So touch.
So lead.

Acknowledgements and Notes

Many of these poems were written in response to hearing stories of people who have lived with bravery, courage and dedication through their troubles. To them, more than thanks are due, but thanks is all I have. *Go raibh míle maith agaibh*, a thousand thanks to you all.

'Hunger strikers', 'The Sash' and 'This is the word of the lord' were written as part of the Through the Green Gate programme, designed by Paul Hutchinson and Susan McEwen, delivered by Susan McEwen on behalf of the Corrymeela Community and funded by the Community Bridges Programme of the International Fund for Ireland.

'Sacramental' is written for Trent Gilliss.

'Battlefield Bog' is written for Jonny McEwen.

'Same clay' is written for Siobhán McKernan.

'Postcards to the centre' and 'The Pedagogy of Conflict' were written for gatherings at the Corrymeela Centre where The Olive Tree Project (based in City University,

London) met with peace practitioners, politicians and storytellers in the north of Ireland.

'go to hell' was written for Jonny Clark and first appeared in *Discovering The Spirit in the City* (London, Continuum, 2010).

'Babel' was written in response to an art exhibition by Paul Gray and was a joint project between Gilnahirk Presbyterian and St Colmcille's Catholic parishes in East Belfast during Good Relations Week 2009. The project was jointly sponsored by Belfast City and Castlereagh Borough Councils.

'Childsplay' and 'Telling Secrets' were written for the Faith and Conflict conference run by Youth With A Mission Belfast at the Corrymeela Centre in the summer of 2007.

'Firewhiskey' was written for Fr Gerry Reynolds of Clonard Monastery.

'In the beginning', 'In the beginning, part II', 'Mixed marriage', and 'Conversation starters' were written as part of the Re:Mapping project, designed by Jonny McEwen and Paul Hutchinson.

'Men in a war', 'Girl in a blitz' and 'Mother praying while the blitz rained down' were written as part of East Belfast Mission's commemoration project marking 70 years since the Belfast Blitz in 1942.

'And isn't it true for all of us', 'Troubles in the concrete and field', 'Clan' and 'Once upon a timebomb' were written for the Pilgrim Trail project, designed by Paul Hutchinson and led by Susan McEwen of the Corrymeela Community in 2005–2006.

'Ikon' was written as part of an Ikon art exhibition in the Belfast Waterfront art space. The acrostic words that form the structure are the five words central to the Ikon crowd in Belfast.

'We are not the same' was written for IDAHO day (International Day Against HOmophobia) during a residency with the Uniting Church of Australia in 2013. Grateful thanks to Cheryl Lawrie, David Pargeter and the Victorian and Tasmanian Synod of the UCA for this residency.

'Shaking Hands' was written in response to an event designed and hosted by Co-operation Ireland where Martin McGuinness, the deputy First Minister of the Northern Ireland Assembly, and Queen Elizabeth II shook hands for the first time.

Grateful thanks to the funders behind these projects. The Special European Union Programmes Body who funded Peace II and Peace III projects, the International Fund for Ireland, the Corrymeela Community, East Belfast Mission, Co-operation Ireland, the Glencree Centre for Peace and Reconciliation, the Community Relations Council, Belfast City Council and Castlereagh Borough Council.

Finally, many many thanks to Christine Smith and all her colleagues at Canterbury Press.